To Great Aunty Vi
Love from
Laura
xx

May 1996.

CW00952475

Beautiful
Cotswold Country

A LAND OF STREAM AND STONE

Described by S. P. B. Mais

Painted by H. Sylvester Stannard R.A.
and George F. Nicholls

SALMON

Published by
J Salmon Limited
100 London Road, Sevenoaks,
Kent TN13 1BB

First edition 1995
Designed by the Salmon Studio

ISBN 1 898435 40 5

Printed in England by
J Salmon Limited, Tubs Hill Works
Sevenoaks, Kent

WILLERSEY

Coloured Illustrations

UPPER SLAUGHTER

FOREWORD

THE COTSWOLDS can proudly claim to be the most unspoilt part of the English countryside. Its scores of hamlets and villages nestling into the folds of the wolds are all built of the local limestone of a warm yellow colour that has been saturated with the sun of centuries and possess stone roofs which are as grey as a pigeon's feathers. They are so much in harmony with their surroundings that they give the impression of having grown naturally out of the hillside.

Each village has its own Tudor manor house, with gables, mullioned windows, tall chimneys and generously carved with initials and coats of arms. There is usually a richly decorated Perpendicular church with tall tower, pinnacles and flying buttresses, a large farm with tithe barn and dove-cot, one main street with an inn, a shop or two and a few straggling cottages. Long, low, unmortared stone walls run for miles in all directions enclosing fields where Cotswold sheep have grazed for centuries.

Sheep and wool have been the source of Cotswold prosperity through the ages, and the splendid churches and manor houses are the bequests to posteriry of the rich wool merchants of the 13th, 14th and 15th centuries. The beauty of these valleys and villages is considerably enhanced by a number of enchanting little rills, streams and rivers bearing such sweet-sounding names as Coln, Dikler, Evenlode and Windrush, whose banks are gaily bedecked in spring-time with kingcups, irises and other colourful wild flowers.

STANWAY HOUSE

AROUND THE COTSWOLDS

ONE OF THE BEST centres from which to explore this lovely land is the upland little market town of Stow-on-the-Wold which stands about eight hundred feet up on the ancient Fosse Way and is the meeting place of seven main roads.

It has a fine market square where the annual Horse Fair has been held continuously since 1477. In the middle stands St Edward's Hall which contains a portrait gallery of famous Royalists and Roundheads who fought in the Civil War. The last battle of this campaign in 1646 ended in a hand-to-hand fight in these streets.

St Edward's Grammar School was reconstructed in 1594, and in St Edward's thirteenth century church hundreds of Royalists were imprisoned by the Cromwellians. The ancient stocks have been preserved as well as a tall house with four beautifully fluted columns and the comfortable Talbot Hotel.

After visiting the two neighbouring villages of Lower and Upper Swell on the banks of the Dikler that are gems of Cotswold architecture, we set off northward on our first tour by way of Bourton-on-the-Hill, a lovely upland village of one steep street of grey stone houses, a manor house, a hall and a church.

Further along comes Five Mile Drive with sandstone caves, quarries and larch plantations until at the crest of the wolds, at the "Fish" inn, we look down over the whole superb Vale of Evesham before descending 600 feet to Broadway, the most popular of all Cotswold villages. Its main street on a slope is very wide with grass verges fronting a succession of beautiful high and low gabled houses of Cotswold stone; most picturesque of all is the 16th century "Lygon Arms" Hotel. The ancient church of St Eadburgha has interesting brasses and a fine timbered roof.

Turning south we pass through many-gabled Stanton with its lovely cross, and Stanway with its great manor house and grandiose gateway, to join the infant Windrush at Temple Guiting which has a 12th century church and charming dovecot built into the adjacent manor farmstead. A little further down the river stands Guiting Power, a handful of cottages with gables and dormers standing out at all angles built irregularly round a green and a Norman church that has been beautifully restored. Also on the banks of the Windrush stands Naunton with its 15th century dove-cot containing over a thousand nest-holes.

Following the line of the river we are soon in Bourton-on-the-Water, a little township that is beautified by the crystal clear waters of the Windrush flowing between wide green verges through the middle of the main street with many bridges connecting the fine Cotswold houses with the main road. Behind the Old New Inn is the remarkable Model Village, a complete and accurate reproduction of Bourton on one-tenth scale.

The way home to Stow passes through two of the loveliest villages in the whole of the Cotswolds, Upper and Lower Slaughter. Upper Slaughter Manor House is one of the most beautiful of all Cotswold houses with its steep-pitched roof and long line of twelve gables with dormers. The oldest part of the house is 15th century, but the front is Elizabethan with a two-storeyed Jacobean porch. The village stands in a hillside above the stream and the church has a fine arch leading into it from the Norman tower.

In Lower Slaughter the stream flows down the centre of the village and numerous small bridges, formed of flat stone slabs, span it to enable the cottagers to reach the green-margined road. In the grounds of the manor house is a dove-cot that looks like an enlarged doll's house, with the entrance and exit designed as cupolas.

THE STOCKS, STOW-ON-THE-WOLD

THE CROSS, CONDICOTE

BOURTON-ON-THE-HILL

HARVESTING NEAR WILLERSEY

THE CROSS, SAINTBURY

OLD HOUSES AT BROADWAY

THE VILLAGE GREEN, BROADWAY

THE CROSS, STANTON

DOWN THE HILL, WINCHCOMBE

BOURTON-ON-THE-WATER

THE RIVER WINDRUSH, BOURTON-ON-THE-WATER

BOURTON-ON-THE-WATER

LOWER SLAUGHTER

THE MILL, LOWER SLAUGHTER

UPPER SLAUGHTER

SUDELEY CASTLE

OUR SECOND TOUR takes us north and east of Stow by way of quiet Adlestrop, about which Edward Thomas wrote a very beautiful poem, and Aylesford, once the home of Warren Hastings. Nearby stands Chastleton House, a magnificent 17th century mansion built by Walter Jones, a Witney wool merchant. There is a grand tithe barn that looks like a banqueting hall and a delightful little dove-cot raised on four arches with high gables and a central cupola.

On the summit of a nearby ridge overlooking Long Compton are the Rollright Stones, the Stonehenge of the Cotswolds, which consist of a circle of 27 stones; a group of Whispering Knights and the King Stone. These, according to legend, were soldiers of an invading army that were turned into stone by a witch. Just south of the stones stands Chipping Norton, an ancient market town with an exceptionally wide street, a Town Hall built in the classical style and much more picturesque Guildhall. The 17th century almshouses stand near the Perpendicular church which has an hexagonal porch and two north aisles.

A few miles north of Chipping Norton by way of Moreton-in-Marsh, we reach Chipping Campden, one of the loveliest of all Cotswold villages. The curved medieval High Street is a gem, full of beautiful houses with fluted stone columns, stone doorways and stone-flagged narrow alleys to covered-in courts leading to stone-walled gardens. In the middle stands the Market Hall propped up on tall pillars with an arched roof of curved beams. Specially notable is the gabled house of William Grevel, the 15th century wool merchant, with stone-arched doorways and large orieled windows.

On the way up to the magnificent tall-towered Perpendicular church we pass the low, gabled, stone almshouses and the walls of the ancient mansion with square dove-cots and outhouses, its deco-rated stone chimneys carved in spirals. An avenue of elms leads into the very light and lofty church which contains a huge marble monument of Sir Baptist Hicks and fine brasses of Grevel, and Lethenard, who was Mayor in 1467.

South of Chipping Norton we join the valley of the Evenlode at Shipton-under-Wychwood, a village of lovely gardens and a stone inn called the "Shaven Crown". The church, which has a tower and spire, contains a 15th century stone pulpit and font and interesting monuments including a palimpsest. We follow the river down to Charlbury, which possesses two pleasant inns, the "Bull" and the "Bear" and two imposing country mansions on the fringe of the ancient forest of Wychwood which is mentioned in Domesday and was formerly full of deer. Wychwood Fair used to be an occasion of great jollity for all the surrounding countryside.

Following the course of the Evenlode we are soon in Woodstock, for centuries a royal hunting box and long famous for the manufacture of hand-made gloves. Henry II built a house here for Fair Rosamund Clifford, and the Black Prince was born in the borough which still has a Mayor and Corporation. The "Bear" is an ancient hotel with a high reputation and the Church and Town Hall are well worth visiting.

Blenheim Palace was built in the Italian Renaissance style in the early part of the 18th century at a cost of £250,000 by Sir John Vanbrugh and given to John Churchill, first Duke of Marlborough, for services rendered to the nation in Europe. It stands above a large lake, the haunt of the great crested grebe, and boasts a magnificent park with very fine trees, enclosed by a wall whose perimeter is ten miles. The Palace and gardens are open to the public for part of the year and the park all the year round. Sir Winston Churchill was born in Blenheim Palace, and is buried at nearby Bladon.

We now turn south-west to join the river Windrush at Witney, famous for centuries for the making of blankets, a typical Cotswold town of wide streets and gabled stone houses, important enough in the Middle Ages to be represented in Parliament by two burgesses. The Butter Cross built in 1683 is a stone-roofed building of great beauty, and beyond it lies a spacious Green leading to the cruciform Parish Church which has a tall spire rising from a pinnacled tower.

West along the banks of the Windrush stand the gracious church and ruined manor house of Minster Lovell, both built by William Lovell in the 15th century. The church which has a fine tower contains the alabaster tomb of William Lovell. The Manor House is supposed to be the scene of the legend of the Mistletoe Bough, in which a young bride hid in a chest and, closing the lid, was never seen again.

A few miles further on stands the beautiful old town of Burford, with one long, very wide, steep street with the grass-margined causeway standing high above the road, and many of its houses gabled and stone-roofed with dormers and stone mullioned windows. At the foot of this street stands the magnificent church with Norman tower and tall tapering spire. It has a very fine south porch, stone vaulted ceiling and a bewildering number of chapels. Adjoining the churchyard are the almshouses founded in 1457 by Warwick the Kingmaker and facing them is the Grammar School, founded in 1571 by Simon Wisdom.

South-west of Burford stands the enchanting village of Bibury on the banks of the Coln, famous for its lovely Arlington Row and picturesque stone Swan Inn, a favourite haunt of anglers. The crystal clear trout stream runs along the main street with rose-filled cottage gardens rising well above the road. At the bottom of the village stands the Saxon church with its many inscriptions to the Sackville family who lived in the gabled Bibury Court, which has embattled bay windows. This is a gracious and lovely Manor House built by Sir Thomas Sackville in 1623.

We follow the Coln valley southwards to the lovely village of Fairford whose pinnacled Perpendicular Church contains some of the finest medieval stained glass windows in the country, given by John Tame, a 15th century wool-stapler. They depict every aspect of the Bible story from Eden to Calvary, but by far the most impressive is the great west window of Judgement Day depicting horned devils scuttling away with the damned thrown across their shoulders and an ogre-like Satan with fish-like head, scaly tail, and jaws between which the lost are devoured by flames. Altogether an unforgettable reminder of the horror of hell.

A few miles west stands Cirencester, one of the most ancient towns in Britain, the meeting point of three of our oldest highways, Ermine Street, the Fosse Way and Akeman Street, known in Roman times as Corinium. It was then second in importance to London. Its outstanding feature today is the magnificent church, originally Norman, with a pinnacled Perpendicular 162 feet high tower built in 1400 and an elaborately decorated two-storeyed south porch of the same period, which for some time served as the Town Hall.

Arlington Row, Bibury

MORETON-IN-MARSH

EBRINGTON NEAR CHIPPING CAMPDEN

OLD HOUSES AT CHIPPING CAMPDEN

THE MARKET HALL, CHIPPING CAMPDEN

A COTSWOLD HOMESTEAD

BURFORD FROM THE TOLSEY

THE RIVER WINDRUSH, BURFORD

BURFORD

THE CHURCH PORCH, NORTHLEACH

A COTSWOLD WATERMEADOW

FAIRFORD MILL AND CHURCH

THE VILLAGE TREE, AMPNEY CRUCIS

CIRENCESTER

THE VILLAGE CROSS, CALMSDEN

WE START OUR THIRD and final tour from Cirencester by way of the Royal Agricultural College, built about 1845, and the spacious and glorious 3,000-acre park created by the first Lord Bathurst (1684-1775), the friend of Alexander Pope, who helped him to transform an open and uncultivated downland into a sort of Versailles with glades, woodland paths and ten broad rides.

Our way lies westward through Sapperton at the head of the Golden Valley, close to the 2½-mile long tunnel through which the now derelict Thames-Severn Canal used to run to join the River Thames at Inglesham a short way above Lechlade. Sapperton has a Queen Anne Church which was built mainly of woodwork from Lord Bathurst's old Manor House.

Further on we come to the glorious Common of Michinhampton, near Rodborough Common and the picturesque village of Amberly with the famous "Bear" inn. From here are wonderful views over the Severn Valley to the Forest of Dean and the Welsh mountains. In addition to its fine Common, Minchinhampton possesses a picturesque Market House, supported on pillars, and a church crowned with a truncated spire trimmed with pinnacles.

Nestling in the foot of the opposite valley lies the town of Nailsworth, with many fine residential houses on its slopes, reached by "Nailsworth Ladder" a hill with a gradient in places of 1 in 2. At the foot of the Golden Valley stands the many-chimneyed, pros-perous manufacturing town of Stroud. It is pleasant to climb out of and away from the narrow, congested, noisy streets of this busy place to the perfect Cotswold hill village of Painswick which contains a quite startling number of beautiful stone gabled houses. Its most remarkable feature is the series of one hundred and four clipped yews that are nearly two hundred years old and pretty well smother the Churchyard. The church which occupies the site of a

Norman church is early 15th century, though it was damaged in the Civil War by Sir William Vavasour who attacked the Roundhead troops when they took refuge in it, and again damaged two hundred years later when the spire was struck by lightning and crashed through the roof into the church. Arguably the two most lovely houses in Painswick are the 16th century stone Court House, and Castle Hale, a 17th century house built on the site of the ancient manor house of Payn FitzJohn.

Above Painswick are two wonderful viewpoints, at Painswick Beacon (922 feet), and Haresfield Beacon, which belongs to the National Trust, and stands about two hundred feet lower, but provides an equally superb view of the whole of the Severn Valley and the Malvern hills. There is a large Roman camp here where some three thousand coins, minted over fifteen hundred years ago, have been unearthed. In the village below there is a Danish or Saxon mound and a monument commemorating the Siege of Gloucester in 1643. Haresfield Church dates back to Norman times, and in the chancel there are two effigies, one of a lady who is dressed in a wimple, dating from 1320.

There is a glorious drive among beech woods along the sides of the steep hill beyond Painswick, which leads by way of the aptly named Paradise to Prinknash Abbey, originally the property of the Benedictine Abbot of Gloucester, and now in the hands of the Benedictine Monks, who used to live at Caldey Island, off the South Wales coast. In 1939 Cardinal Hensley, Archbishop of Westminster, laid the foundations of the new Abbey which was built by the Monks themselves.

High above, and well worth visiting, is Birdlip which has a famous steep hill. Below are miles of lovely woodland known as Buckholt Woods, which lead down to Prinknash again, where we turn right through more woods with grand views of the Severn Valley, till we reach Leckhampton with its lofty church spire. The church was originally Norman, but enlarged in the 14th century and again in 1866. In the north-west corner is the tomb of Sir E. Gifford (died 1330) and his wife. The Giffords lived for centuries at Leckhampton Court, a delightful old house with a 14th century Banqueting Hall.

Near here are the Seven Springs, which are sometimes claimed to be the source of the Thames though they are in fact the source of the River Churn, a headwater of the Thames; the true source of that river is in a meadow at Thames Head beside the Fosse Way near Cirencester.

From Leckhampton we make our final descent into the dignified and charming Regency town of Cheltenham, famous for its Ladies' College and Boys' Public School as well as for its wide tree-lined Parade and the Pitville Gardens with its elegant pump Room.

AUTUMN IN THE COTSWOLDS

AN OLD CORNER, PAINSWICK

A COTSWOLD VILLAGE STORE